INCREDIBLE JOBS YOU'VE (PROBABLY) NEVER HEARD OF

BY: natalie labarre (me)

nosy crow

The GREAT

doctor   lawyer   farmer

First published 2019 by Nosy Crow Ltd
The Crow's Nest, 14 Baden Place, Crosby Row
London, SE1 1YW

www.nosycrow.com

ISBN 978 1 78800 477 0

A CIP catalogue record for this book is available from the British Library.

Printed in China.
Papers used by Nosy Crow are made from wood
grown in sustainable forests.

1 3 5 7 9 8 6 4 2

Natalie Labarre, who made this book, is an
ILLUSTRATOR and **ANIMATOR**. These two jobs mean
she gets to draw and tell stories all day for adverts,
films and her own personal work. Natalie is obsessed
with unusual jobs because she was so relieved when
she finally found out that you can draw for a living!

HALL of JOBS

teacher

chef

athlete

pilot

Do you know what you want to do
WHEN YOU GROW UP?
I bet you get asked that a lot, right?

You might already have one of these jobs in mind . . .
THE CLASSICS! And these are great . . .

But did you know that there are ALL SORTS of incredible jobs out there that you've probably never heard of?

One of them might be just right for you!

SKYSCRAPER WINDOW CLEANERS need more than a ladder to reach these high-rise windows. They work suspended in mid-air almost 300 metres up — except when it's too windy!

For the most expensive beef in the world, **COW MASSAGERS** in Japan make sure their cows are as relaxed as possible by giving them regular massages.

161

WELCOME

Can you spot people doing these jobs?
Find them again later in the book
to learn more about them.

- Professional Queuer
- Rubbish Detective
- Corpse Farmer
- Golfball Diver
- Ski Patroller
- Sloth Nanny
- Waterslide Tester
- Bicycle Fisher
- Nautical Cowboy
- Smoke Jumper

FUNERAL CLOWNS are paid to lighten the mood on difficult days. Wearing bright clothes and playing tricks, they help people to remember their loved ones with a smile.

Using a feather duster, this **DINOSAUR DUSTER** keeps the dinosaur bones in the Natural History Museum spotless. They're 145 million years old so he has to be extremely careful. No shaky hands!

MUSEUM

Believe it or not, Queen Elizabeth II owns all of the swans in the UK! Every year, a **WARDEN OF THE SWANS** catches each one living on the River Thames, checks their health, marks them and sets them free. This ceremony is called Swan Upping.

There are **11 swans** missing! Can you find them in this scene?

TOPIARY ARTISTS have been around for thousands of years. They use special tools to sculpt bushes into fancy shapes and their work can be found anywhere — from castle gardens to Disneyland!

Jobs can come in ALL SHAPES AND SIZES — it just depends on what you're looking for!

What about something . . .

…CREATIVE?

One at a time, a **WIG MAKER** sews thousands of real human hairs into a very fine net that is the shape of the soon-to-be wearer's head. Then it's styled just the way they like it. The new hairdos can sit on the heads of anyone from stage actors to cancer patients.

…METICULOUS?

At some lakes during spawning season (when fish lay their eggs), you can catch a **FISH COUNTER** carefully keeping track of life underwater. Wildlife experts record the numbers of different species to help prevent any of them getting wiped out by over-fishing.

…MYSTERIOUS?

CRYPTOZOOLOGISTS try to find evidence of creatures from myths and legends that others don't think are real, like Bigfoot or the Loch Ness Monster. Actual zoologists call their work 'pseudoscience', as it can't be proven by scientific fact — but don't tell them that!

Coconuts for horse hooves, flapping gloves for bird's wings — these are just some of the tricks a **FOLEY ARTIST** might use to record realistic sound effects for Hollywood films. The method is named after famous sound effect artist Jack Foley, who invented it in the 1920s.

...DANGEROUS?

If found, even a 100-year-old bomb, landmine, or grenade left over from a long-ago war could explode at any time. An **UNEXPLODED ORDNANCE TECHNICIAN** specialises in safely investigating and removing any dangerous unexploded devices. Phew!

...OR FABULOUS?

Can you spot the difference between a quickly fading fad and a trend that's here to stay? Leave it to a **TREND SPOTTER** to always know what's cool and what's not. This information can be worth billions to the most cutting-edge brands.

With some jobs . . .

. . . you'll get to T R A V E L

You might have heard of cowboys moving cattle across prairies, but a **NAUTICAL COWBOY** will help ship livestock across oceans to different parts of the world. Yee-haw! These sea cowboys make sure the animals have enough food, water and fresh air for their long journey around the globe.

. . . you'll meet
S U P E R   I N T E R E S T I N G   C O - W O R K E R S

Submarine crews often work under the sea for 90 days at a time, so luckily they have talented **SUBMARINE CHEFS** to feed them. They tickle the crew's taste buds with delightful dishes designed to spice up their otherwise long and sometimes dull time underwater.

SS MOO

. . . you'll learn NEW SKILLS

Have you ever heard of milking a snake? **SNAKE MILKERS** spend years training to carefully collect deadly venom from poisonous snakes by making them bite into a rubber covered pot! The poison can be used for many things, such as medical research and making anti-venom to treat snake bites. A patient suffering from a snake bite might last as little as two hours if they're not treated in time, so get milking!

Some jobs happen
high above...

Mount Rushmore in South Dakota, USA, is a huge stone sculpture of past American presidents and **CRACK FILLERS** work to stop the historic landmark from crumbling. The repair team use silicone sealant to fill cracks in the stone almost 2,000 metres high. Even enormous stone faces need a little facial now and again!

You don't look a day over two hundred, Mr President!

. . . others operate
way underground.

In Tokyo, Japan, the trains are so crowded during morning and evening rush-hours that they have white-gloved **TRAIN PUSHERS** or 'oshiya' to actually push people on board. The oshiya pack the trains tight and make sure nobody gets caught in the doors. It's a tight squeeze for people hoping to get to work on time as the trains are filled to almost twice their capacity!

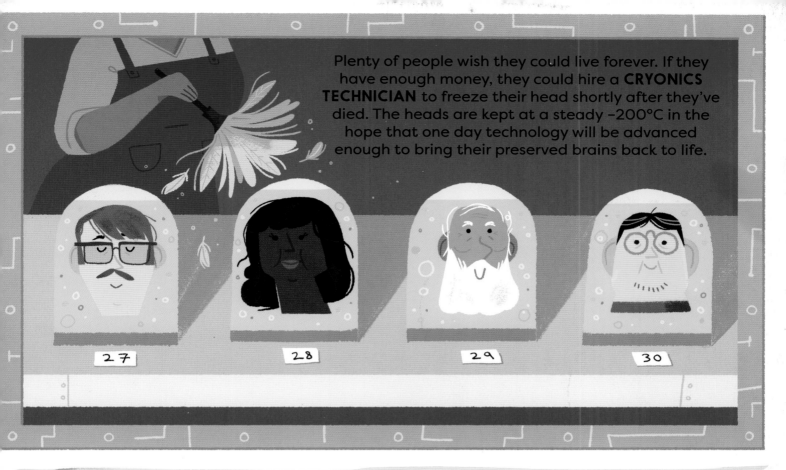

Plenty of people wish they could live forever. If they have enough money, they could hire a **CRYONICS TECHNICIAN** to freeze their head shortly after they've died. The heads are kept at a steady −200°C in the hope that one day technology will be advanced enough to bring their preserved brains back to life.

27   28   29   30

Who better to ask about the wonders of preservation than a **MUMMY EXPERT**? They dedicate their lives to knowing all there is to know about these wrapped-up bundles of history. In 1994, a mummy expert and leading Egyptologist mummified a real human in the ancient Egyptian way — the first person to do so in 2,000 years. YIKES!

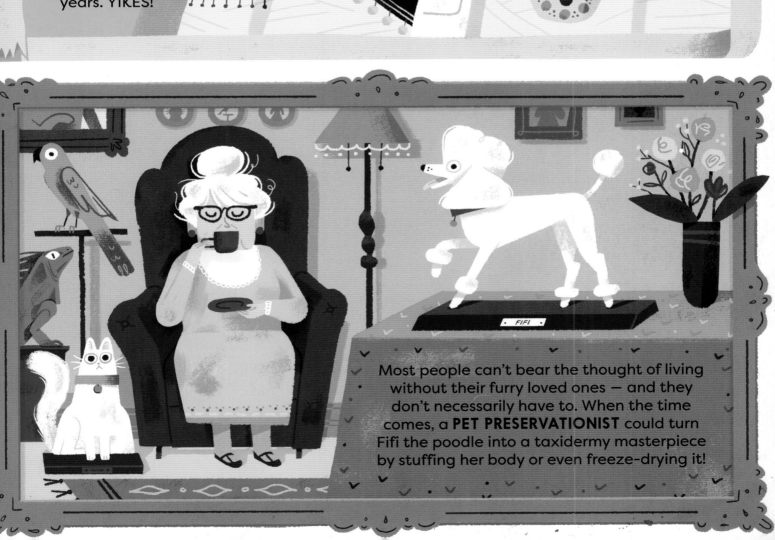

FIFI

Most people can't bear the thought of living without their furry loved ones — and they don't necessarily have to. When the time comes, a **PET PRESERVATIONIST** could turn Fifi the poodle into a taxidermy masterpiece by stuffing her body or even freeze-drying it!

Too grisly? Fair enough. How about some quirky jobs for the TALENTED WRITERS amongst you?

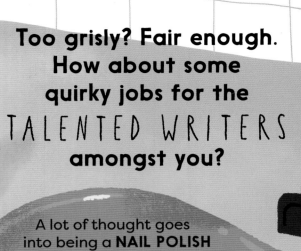

A lot of thought goes into being a **NAIL POLISH NAMER**, which is actually often a group effort. The team behind a new nail colour will come up with ideas together; even taking trips to find inspiration for the perfect name. It's got to be catchy because memorable names can boost sales by a lot!

CONGRAT ULATIONS YOU'RE OLD

GREETINGS! — HERE'S A CARD!

A feeling is an idea with roots.

According to **FORTUNE COOKIE WRITERS**, a good fortune has got to be thought-provoking, a little surprising, but also vague AND relatable to whoever ends up opening it. Not easy! But someone has to come up with the messages for the 3 billion cookies made each year!

Laura from down the hall doesn't actually like your new shirt.

Eat your vegetables — or else!

Ghoul Grey

MONKEY SNACKS

SNOW DAY

= YOU'RE =

GRAPE !!

What better way to show your true feelings to a loved one than by having a complete stranger write something for you? A **GREETINGS CARD WRITER** comes up with clever or thoughtful messages so you don't have to. Thank goodness! Full-time writers might produce from two to twenty cards per week!

A **CROSSWORD PUZZLE WRITER** can spend anywhere from a week to a month making the perfect puzzle for cruciverbalists (otherwise known as people who love solving crosswords) to figure out — go figure!

I
BANANA
C
R
E
COOKIE DINOW
D W
I
JOBS B
L
ELEPHANT
N STR

Some jobs sound like fun and games. A **TOY DESIGNER** needs a big imagination to come up with toys that everybody wants. They must have good mechanical skills and an expert knowledge of how children play.

The job of a **TOY BREAKER** is to take all of that hard work and smash it to bits! It may be messy, but it's important for making playtime safe. Toys are tested to see how long they last and reports are written about any potential dangers.

Imagine if it was your job to live in paradise! **ISLAND CARETAKERS** look after incredible places to make sure they don't get ruined. Some islands are super luxurious, while others are a little wilder and call for outdoorsy skills. Either way, you can't beat ending the workday with a sunset on the beach.

The most-fun-job award probably goes to **WATERSLIDE TESTERS**. Water parks and travel companies actually pay people to test some of the craziest rides around the world. Testers check for safety, speed, creative features and there's a scale to rate the 'splash factor' and 'adrenaline levels'.

The Nose Dive

Rapunzel's Escape

The Medusa

Looking for even more
of A THRILL?

When a forest fire is impossible to reach, specialised firefighters called **SMOKE JUMPERS** are called in to leap out of helicopters and fight the blazes by parachute. Working in small groups and wearing extremely heavy equipment, smoke jumpers can spend days putting out the fire!

Or maybe you'd rather CHILL?

PROFESSIONAL SLEEPERS get paid to snooze —
for scientific research, to test new sleep medicine
or even to report on new sleep products. It might
sound dreamy, but it's not always! In 2017, NASA
ran a study that would help to keep astronauts safe
in space — they paid 12 volunteers to stay in a bed
tilted upside down for 30 days straight!

Are you a particularly PATIENT person?

Oh perfect! Have you ever thought of becoming a **TORTOISE WALKER**? In New York, USA, a job was advertised to look after a tortoise named Henry, taking him on walks and cleaning up after him. According to his owner, the walker had to be good with animals and with people too, as everyone would want to stop and chat with their curious neighbour.

If you're patient and you also happen to love cleaning, an **IMAX SCREEN CLEANER** position could be a great fit. It takes about eight hours to clean dust, food and even spit off the 16 x 22 metre screen. That's as tall as a seven-storey building!

Are you that person who sings Christmas songs all year round? Do you wear a Christmas jumper to go grocery shopping? Well, you're going to love this! At a big supermarket in Wrexham, in the UK, you can get a job as a **CHRISTMAS LIGHT UNTANGLER** (if you can untangle three metres of lights in under three minutes!).

As a **PROFESSIONAL QUEUER**, you could get paid to stand in line to buy the latest gadget or food craze for someone else. It could take minutes or even hours. By the time you get to the front of the queue, you should be able to afford as many 'conuts' as you want!

HOME OF THE conut

Third time in this queue today. I'm going to be rich!

What about joining the Golden Gate Bridge's painting squad? In San Francisco, USA, a team of **BRIDGE PAINTERS** look after its protective orange coat. With 600,000 rivets to paint by hand in one tower alone, it's no small task, but the glorious view probably makes up for it.

Perhaps you are more of a VISUAL person?
What about a job with a little
MORE COLOUR?

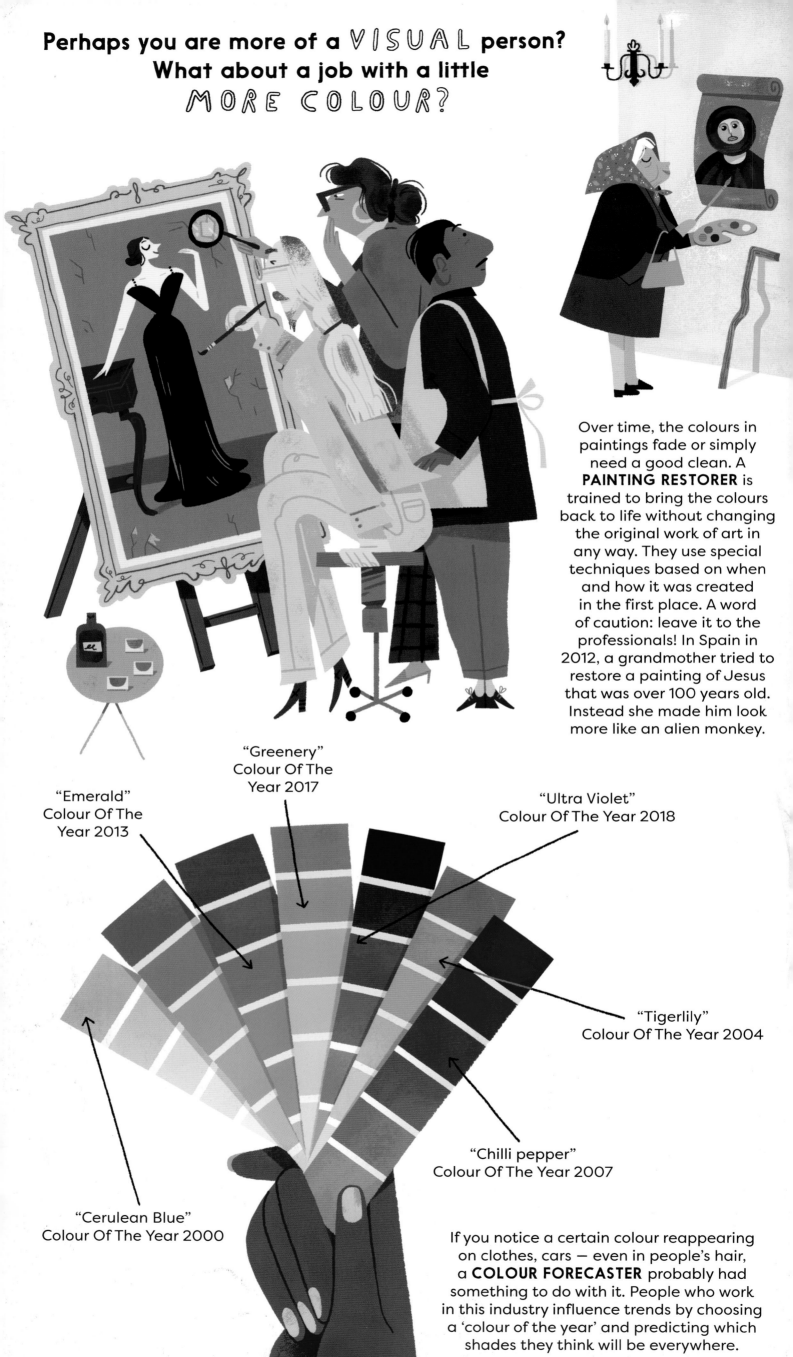

Over time, the colours in paintings fade or simply need a good clean. A **PAINTING RESTORER** is trained to bring the colours back to life without changing the original work of art in any way. They use special techniques based on when and how it was created in the first place. A word of caution: leave it to the professionals! In Spain in 2012, a grandmother tried to restore a painting of Jesus that was over 100 years old. Instead she made him look more like an alien monkey.

"Greenery"
Colour Of The
Year 2017

"Emerald"
Colour Of The
Year 2013

"Ultra Violet"
Colour Of The Year 2018

"Tigerlily"
Colour Of The Year 2004

"Cerulean Blue"
Colour Of The Year 2000

"Chilli pepper"
Colour Of The Year 2007

If you notice a certain colour reappearing on clothes, cars — even in people's hair, a **COLOUR FORECASTER** probably had something to do with it. People who work in this industry influence trends by choosing a 'colour of the year' and predicting which shades they think will be everywhere.

Every colour has a distinct personality and can affect the way we feel. That's why it was so important for these clients to hire a **COLOUR CONSULTANT** when redecorating their house. By getting to know the couple and the mood they wanted to create in this room, their consultant expertly chose a colour scheme that made their house feel more like a home. Even Princess Pooch loves it!

In some countries, elephants play an important role in religious festivals and special occasions. It's an **ELEPHANT DRESSER**'s job to create beautiful, colourful costumes for the glamorous giants to wear when they take part in special days.

One of these baby chicks is male — the other is female. Can you tell them apart? If you've got it right, congratulations! You're a natural born **CHICKEN SEXER**. It's very difficult to tell the difference because they look exactly the same on the outside. So large chicken farms will use sexers to tell males and females apart. The only way to check is by giving each chick a gentle squeeze and peeking inside their bottom! Ewwwwwwww.

If you're a caring kind of person (and chicken poo sounds seriously icky), then you'd probably prefer being a **SLOTH NANNY**, giving love and care to orphaned sloths. They need a lot of looking after, so your job would be getting them ready to be released back into the wild. Who wouldn't want to spend all day taking care of adorable baby sloths?

-Heidi-
The cross-eyed opossum

LASSIE

DOLLY

-Mr Ed-

Thelma and Elise

PIZZA RAT

Eddie

LONESOME -George-

CHOUPETTE

BABE

SONYA The slow loris

SINGING JACK

Bubbles

Are you always staring at other people's pets? Well, that creepiness could turn into a career! An **ANIMAL TALENT AGENT** searches for cute animals that belong in front of a camera. From dogs and cats to more exotic species, an agent can provide trained animals of all types for film, television, photoshoots, theatre and more.

Can you guess what a **SPECIALIST FOR BIOLOGICAL AVIATION SAFETY** does for a living? Give up? That's the official title for an airport scarecrow — a real person whose job it is to make sure birds don't get in the way of landing or departing planes, for both animal and human safety. If there are birds on the runway, the scarecrow needs to rush to the scene and make a lot of noise to hopefully frighten them away.

Being cramped in space for long periods of time is no easy ride. That's why astronauts rely on a **SPACE PSYCHOLOGIST** to keep track of their mental health before, during and after every space mission. While in space, there are many home comforts that an astronaut might miss (like toilets and showers), but a space psychologist will talk them through it.

A **SPACESUIT DESIGN ENGINEER** gets the crew looking their best just in case we make contact with another planet. It's important to make a good first impression! Just kidding! The designer mostly focuses on how the suit will work as a piece of equipment for life in space, but it still looks pretty awesome, too.

The real-life job of an **ASTROBIOLOGIST** is to look for aliens, to figure out how Earth came to be in the first place and to find a new planet for humans to move to once we ruin this one. No pressure! So far, Mars is looking good!

Once in space, any smells inside the shuttle get stronger and stronger. That's because it's such a small space and it's very hot — a bit like when you're in a car for a long time. Since it wouldn't be a bright idea to roll down a window, NASA uses a **CHIEF SNIFFER** whose job it is to smell-check anything that'll be on the ship. He's taken part in more than 850 smell missions since 1974!

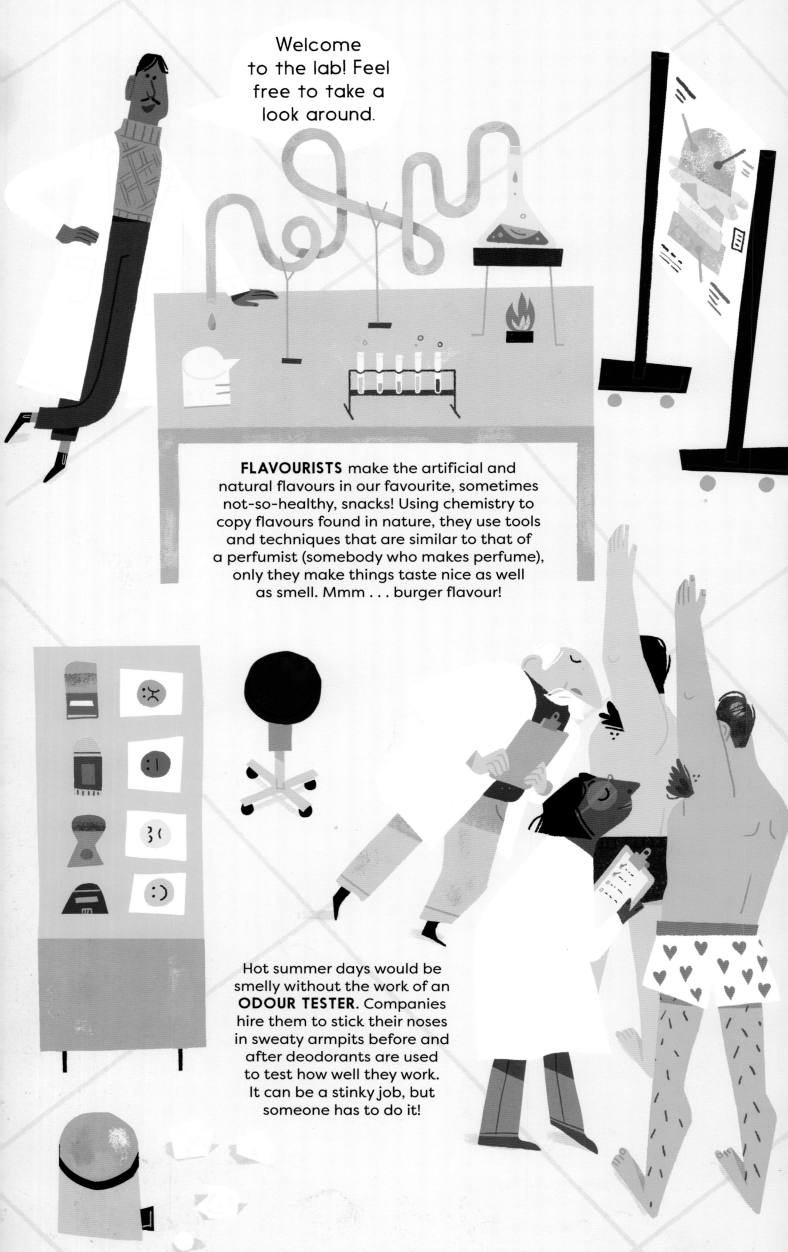

Welcome to the lab! Feel free to take a look around.

FLAVOURISTS make the artificial and natural flavours in our favourite, sometimes not-so-healthy, snacks! Using chemistry to copy flavours found in nature, they use tools and techniques that are similar to that of a perfumist (somebody who makes perfume), only they make things taste nice as well as smell. Mmm . . . burger flavour!

Hot summer days would be smelly without the work of an **ODOUR TESTER**. Companies hire them to stick their noses in sweaty armpits before and after deodorants are used to test how well they work. It can be a stinky job, but someone has to do it!

Now you might think this looks a bit odd, but this **FACE FEELER** is actually hard at work. Also known as a sensory scientist, they touch people's faces to test how well different skincare products work — everything from face cleansers and moisturisers to razors and peels.

Picky eaters beware! **TASTE TESTERS** analyse products with their expert tongues, from medical studies where you might get paid to eat only fast food for three months, to testing food that's not even real food, like dog food! Tasting requires a lot of concentration and you'll need to take good care of your 10,000 taste buds, resting between courses and avoiding anything too spicy or salty.

Another scientifically smelly job is a **BREATH ODOUR EVALUATOR**, who takes a whiff of somebody's breath before and after they have used a product, like chewing gum or mouthwash. Their job is to figure out the difference and rate the smell each time.

Whether you're in a SMELLY LAB or BUSY WORKSHOP, the right setting is key to a job well done!

Can you match these five people to their WORKSPACES?

"Can you think of anything more beautiful than making something old as good as new again? Neither can I — as a matter of fact, I transform things for a living! Artists and writers send me their tools through the post, I'll freshen them up and send them back, always with shavings as a 'certificate of sharpening'."

A

"Oh, don't mind me . . . I'm not breaking the law. I'm just breaking into a system. But don't worry, it's my job! Companies pay me to check for problems or weak spots and then fix them before any real thieves give it a try."

B

"EYE can see you! I just love that joke, but being hilarious is not all I do! I specialise in creating fake body parts for people who need them. I start by taking measurements, and then I make a model and paint it as realistically as possible. SEE what I mean . . .?"

C

"I can stomach the most squeamish of snacks! My hard work goes into those disgusting moments on TV that might make you look away. I am hired to try things out — several times — just to make sure they're safe for celebrity challenges."

D

"If you see someone in trouble on the slopes, you'd better give me a call! In an emergency, I rescue people that have gone missing on the mountain and can provide first aid. Sometimes I even get to trigger avalanches so nobody else accidentally does. It's . . . pretty COOL!"

E

Some workplaces are WETTER than others. It's amazing what you can find when you're FISHING for it . . .

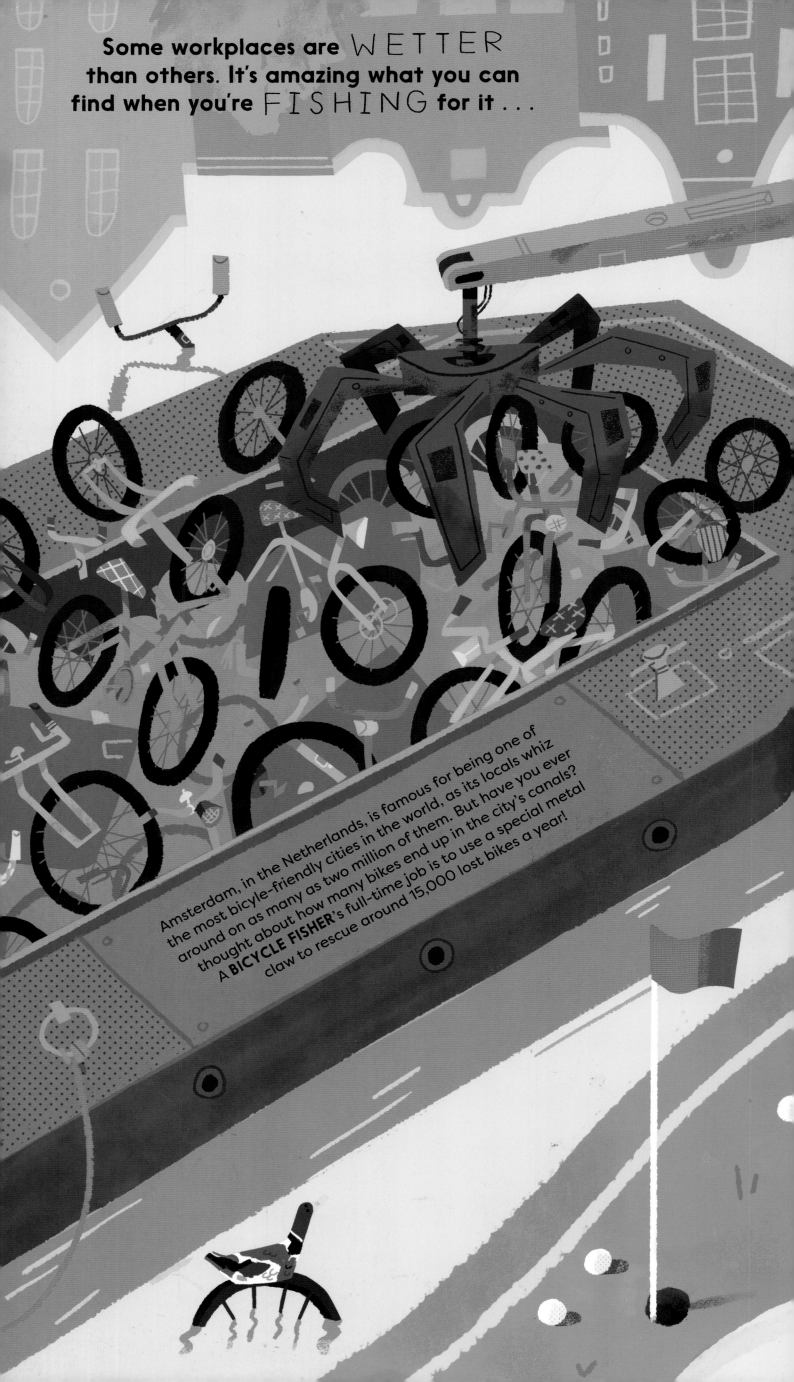

Amsterdam, in the Netherlands, is famous for being one of the most bicycle-friendly cities in the world, as its locals whiz around on as many as two million of them. But have you ever thought about how many bikes end up in the city's canals? A **BICYCLE FISHER**'s full-time job is to use a special metal claw to rescue around 15,000 lost bikes a year!

I like to think that bikes make for much better wishes than coins . . .

Here's a completely different type of fishing . . . **GOLF BALL DIVERS** pay a fee to golf courses so that they are allowed to spend eight to ten hours a day plundering their ponds. That's because these professional recyclers can make a lot of money cleaning, packaging and reselling any golf balls they can find lurking in the deep water. Just watch out for alligators!

There are **6 golf balls** missing! Can you help find them in the pages of this book?

ANSWERS: TRAIN PUSHER, TOY DESIGNER, PROFESSIONAL SLEEPER, SPACE PSYCHOLOGIST, ODOUR TESTER, MIME ARTIST.

If you don't mind fishing through other people's rubbish, you could be someone who ENFORCES THE RULES...

In Germany, where you'll find some of the world's strictest recycling laws, **RUBBISH DETECTIVES** take their job very seriously. They're always on the lookout for things that aren't thrown away correctly (batteries in the bin? Outrageous!). They dig through bins, check shopping receipts and even question nosy neighbours to find evidence of trash-can crimes!

... or maybe you'd rather be someone who BREAKS THEM!

This guy gets paid to jump on the bed! But he's not monkeying around. **MATTRESS JUMPERS** use their feet to check for any lumps in the filling. They have to be able to feel even a pea-sized lump! They're careful and precise with their jumps — they use a grid pattern so they don't miss a spot.

Meanwhile, this lady plays with her food — professionally! To help sell cheese, supermarkets sometimes hire a live **CHEESE SCULPTOR** to create amazing works of art from cheese. The carved sculptures can also be used at special events, like food festivals. It's brie-lliant!

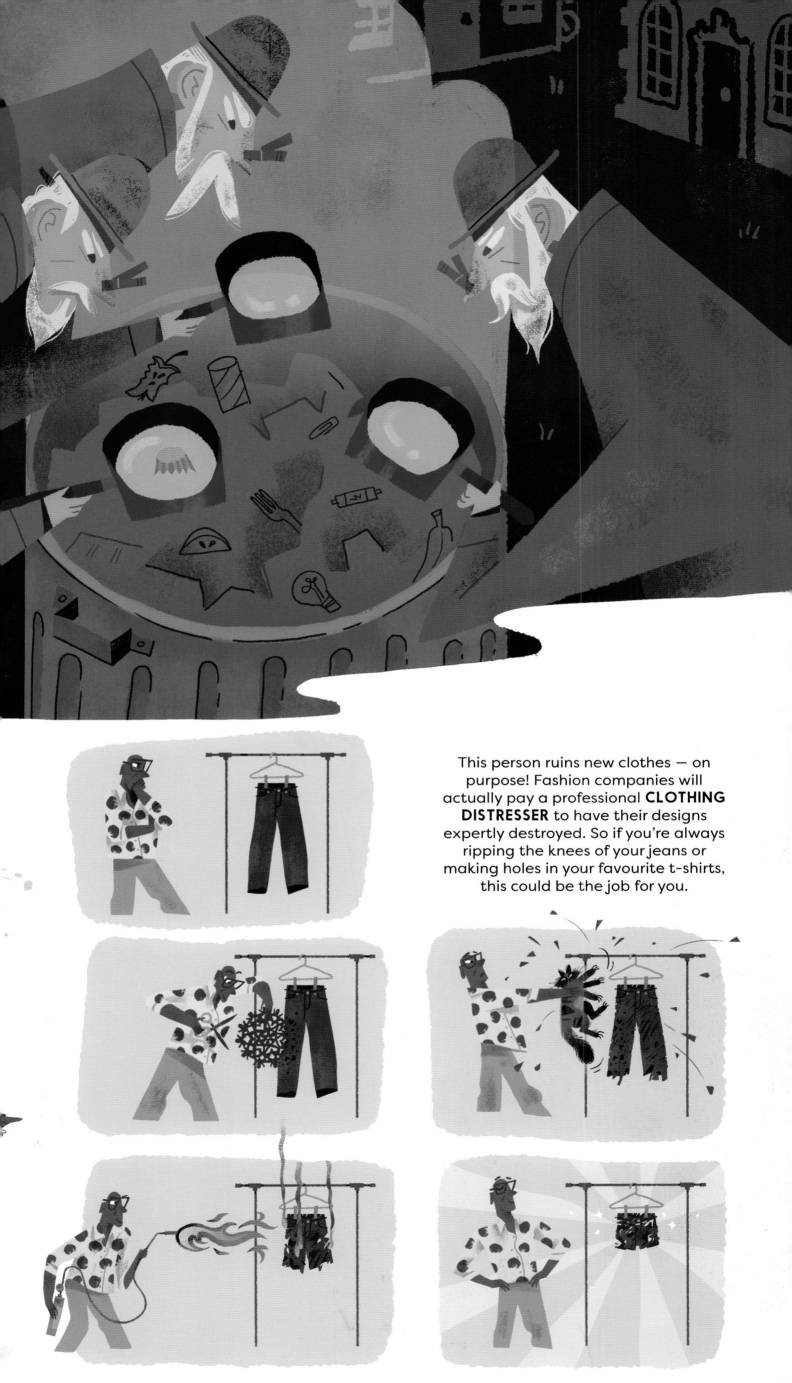

This person ruins new clothes — on purpose! Fashion companies will actually pay a professional **CLOTHING DISTRESSER** to have their designs expertly destroyed. So if you're always ripping the knees of your jeans or making holes in your favourite t-shirts, this could be the job for you.

Hands off THESE CLOTHES!
These people can't do their jobs without them!

Can you guess what they do based on their UNIFORMS?

1

2

3

A

"I wouldn't be able to do my job without my suit. I need to wear it so that animators can use the tracking points to animate crazy features on top of my movements. At least that's what they told me — it could also just be a prank!"

B

"Some say only fools rush in to get married by the king of rock'n'roll, Elvis Presley, but I say — it's now or never! Viva Las Vegas!"

C

"My job dates back almost 200 years. What do I do? I wake up Queen Elizabeth II every morning at 9 am. I stand under her window for about 15 minutes. Works every time."

4

5

6

D

"I've got a head for heights, which is lucky because I wait on tables that are suspended by a crane 50 metres in the air. Guests are strapped in to the flying dinner table like a rollercoaster as I serve them a three-course meal!"

E

"My role is to protect the Pope himself. Dating back to 1506, we're one of the oldest military units in the world. You won't find an army today with a heavier or more complicated uniform: it's made from over 150 pieces, and weighs as much as four bags of sugar!"

F

"It takes weeks to train up a new police dog so they can use their incredible sense of smell to help us search for things. I wear this uniform to protect myself when 'bite sleeve training' — that's when we teach the dog to growl and attack if we're in danger."

Jobs aren't always easy — and sometimes they can even be QUITE EMOTIONAL... literally!

It's usually not a great idea to cry at work, unless you're a **PROFESSIONAL MOURNER** that is. Also called moirologists, these people are hired by the family of someone who has died if they're worried that not many people will be at the funeral. Their job is to cry for aunt Betsy, and pretend that they were friends or family. The mourner is even armed with a fake story in case any real friends and family become suspicious.

Aunt Betsy
Kids x 2
Golfer
Hated cyclists

Putting together a wedding can be stressful. It's no wonder some brides would prefer to trust a **PROFESSIONAL BRIDESMAID** to help with the preparations, rather than their lovely but unqualified friends. Bridesmaids can step in if the maid of honour starts panicking and they can help with things like speech writing, dress shopping or even keeping the peace in the bridal party before the big day.

It can be tough to say sorry, but if you find it easy, you could become a **PROFESSIONAL APOLOGISER**. You could either work as a customer service employee for a large company like an airline, or, in Japan, there are even special apology agencies that can get people to say sorry on your behalf — for anything!

Laughter is contagious. That's why television shows with a live studio audience hire **PROFESSIONAL LAUGHERS** to get everybody going! They can burst out hearty and infectious laughter on command. It's not as easy as it sounds — can you try laughing as loud as you can right this second?

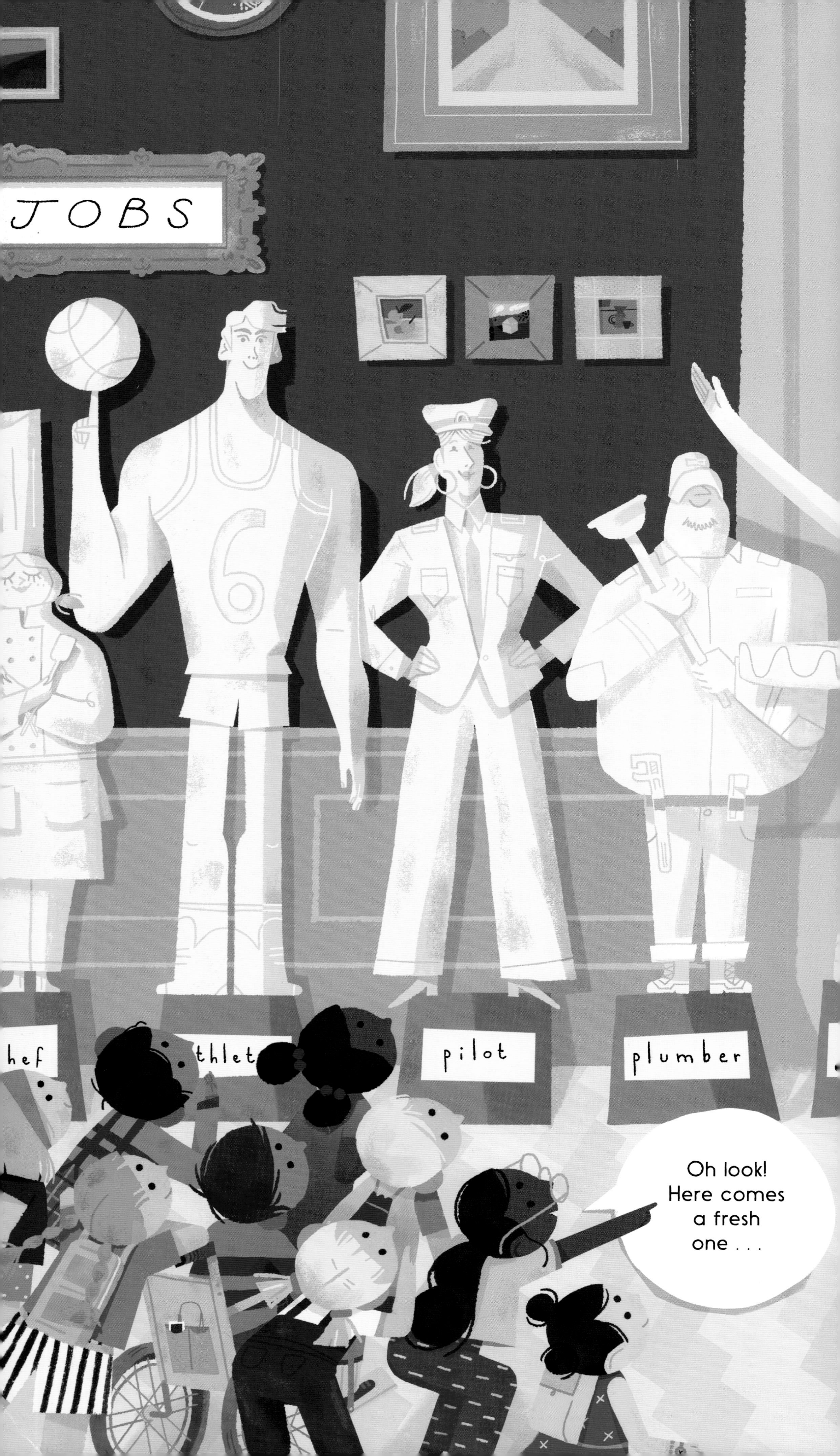

JOBS
hef
thlet
pilot
plumber
Oh look!
Here comes
a fresh
one . . .

Don't worry if you still don't know what your D R E A M   J O B might be.

All the jobs in this book are as U N I Q U E as the people who do them.

The trick to choosing the right job for you, no matter how unusual, is to know yourself.
What do you L O V E to do? Do you know what you're good at?
In a constantly changing world, there are brand new jobs popping up A L L the time!

And of course, you can always change your mind if you want to give something
else a try later on down the line. There are N O   R U L E S !
You don't have to stick with one job forever. Give many things a try to see what you like best!

**And if the job you want doesn't even exist yet,
you could be the one to make it happen!**